Circuits & Conductors

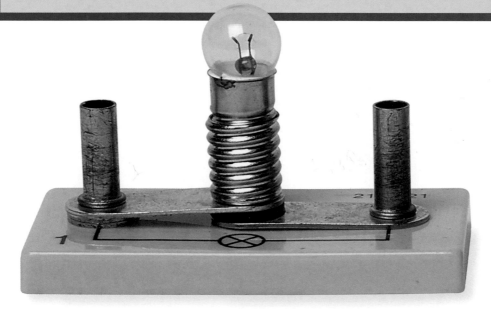

Peter Riley

Smart Apple Media

This book has been published in cooperation with Franklin Watts.

Editor: Rachel Tonkin, Designer: Proof Books, Picture researcher: Diana Morris, Illustrations: Ian Thompson

Picture credits:
Rick Doyle/Corbis: 18; Chet Gordon/Image Works/Topfoto: 23c; Bob Krist/Corbis: 9; Andrew Lambert/Science Photo Library: 25; Jose Fuste Raga/Corbis: 22; Benjamin Rodell/Corbis: 27; Shout Pictures: 20; Sean Sprague/Image Works/Topfoto: 24; Mike Theiss & Jim Reed/Corbis: 16; Anthony Vizard/Eye Ubiquitous/Corbis: 26.

All other images: Andy Crawford

With thanks to our model: Gloria Maddy

Published in the United States by Smart Apple Media
2140 Howard Drive West, North Mankato, Minnesota 56003

Library of Congress Cataloging-in-Publication Data

Riley, Peter D.
Cicuits & conductors / by Peter Riley.
p. cm. — (Essential science)
Includes index.
ISBN-13: 978-1-59920-024-8
1. Electric circuits—Juvenile literature. 2. Electricity—Juvenile literature. 3. Electric conductors—Juvenile literature. 4. Electric insulators and insulation—Juvenile literature. I. Title. II. Title: Circuits and conductors.

TK148.R55 2007
621.319'2—dc22   2006030986

9 8 7 6 5 4 3 2 1

CONTENTS

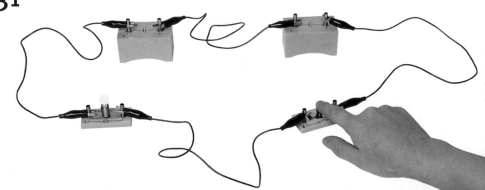

CIRCUITS AND CONDUCTORS

We use electricity for many things. Think of the last time you pressed a switch. Was it to turn off a light, turn on your computer, or change the channel on television? If we want electricity to work for us, we have to let it flow as a current. Materials that allow electricity to flow through them are called conductors.

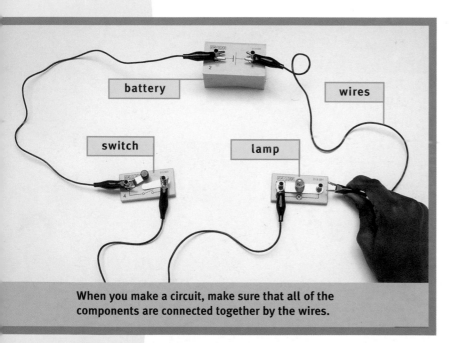

When you make a circuit, make sure that all of the components are connected together by the wires.

battery

switch

lamp

wires

A simple circuit

Electricity flows in a loop called a circuit. The items that are linked together to make a circuit are called components. There is no beginning or end to a circuit, but if there is a gap between any component, the electricity stops flowing and the circuit does not work. A simple circuit can be made with a battery, a switch, a lamp, and three wires, as shown in the picture.

A battery contains a store of electrical energy. When the battery is connected to a circuit, it pushes a current of electricity around the circuit.

The wires are made of metal coated in plastic. Metals allow electricity to pass through them. They are conductors.

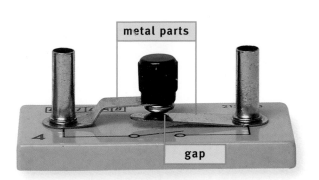

metal parts

gap

A switch has two metal parts with a gap between them that can be opened or closed. When the gap is closed, electricity flows through the circuit. When the gap is opened, electricity cannot flow.

filament

A lamp has a metal wire called a filament in it that can conduct electricity. When the electrical current flows through the filament, the filament glows and the lamp shines.

Household circuits

There are many circuits around you in the walls and ceilings of rooms that lead to lights and outlets. The electricity that flows through these circuits comes from a power station. In a power station, generators produce huge amounts of electrical energy. They make larger, more powerful currents than batteries make. You must never perform experiments using household circuits. It is dangerous.

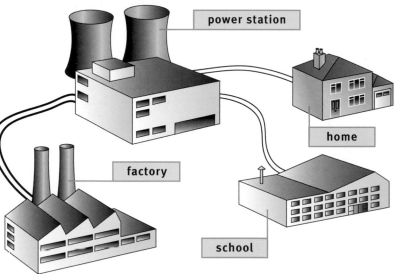

power station

home

factory

school

The electricity from a power station travels on overhead cables and underground cables to the circuits in homes, schools, and factories.

Use the data

When scientists do experiments, they make observations and record them. This information is called data. It may be in a table, bar graph, or line graph. Look around your home. Make a list of all of the different electrical devices in each room and record it in a bar chart. How does your data compare?

Answers to questions in this book are on page 31.

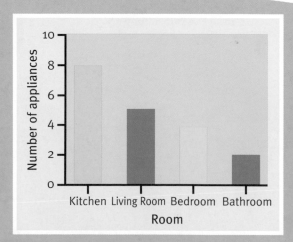

BATTERIES AND CELLS

A battery is a portable source of electricity. You can put it in a flashlight or in an electric toothbrush and carry it around with you. Most of the electrical components we call batteries are cylinder shaped. In science, these are called cells.

A cell

This diagram shows the inside of a cell.

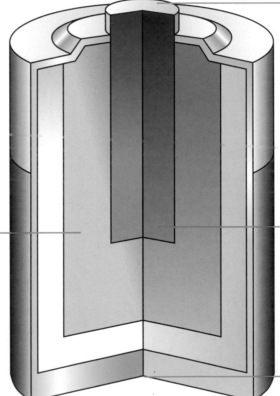

POSITIVE TERMINAL
This metal cap is called the positive terminal. There may be a plus (+) sign close to it on the case.

CHEMICAL PASTE
This is a paste that contains chemicals that make electricity.

CARBON ROD
This carbon rod helps in the electricity-making process.

NEGATIVE TERMINAL
This end of the cell is called the negative terminal. There may be a negative (-) sign close to it on the case.

A cell provides electricity to make this calculator work.

Connecting wires

When a cell is connected to a circuit, one end of a wire must touch the positive terminal and one end of another wire must touch the negative terminal. The current travels around the circuit from the negative terminal to the positive terminal.

Batteries

Two or more cells can be placed in a circuit to increase the push of the current. The cells must be placed with the positive terminal of one cell next to the negative terminal of the next cell. A row of two or more cells in line forms a battery. Some large batteries are box shaped. They contain cells joined together.

Why cells die

Chemicals in the paste inside a cell take part in an irreversible change as they generate electrical energy. This means that they are eventually used up, which is why cells and batteries die.

Here are five cells of different sizes. Inside the blue container is a battery of two cells.

The power of a cell

The power of a cell to send electricity around a circuit is measured in volts. The symbol for this is V, and the power in volts is shown on the side of the cell. For example, a cell that has a power of one and a half volts will have 1.5 V written on its side.

Connecting cells

In which circuits would the bulb light up if you press the switch?

A

B

C

D

SYMBOLS

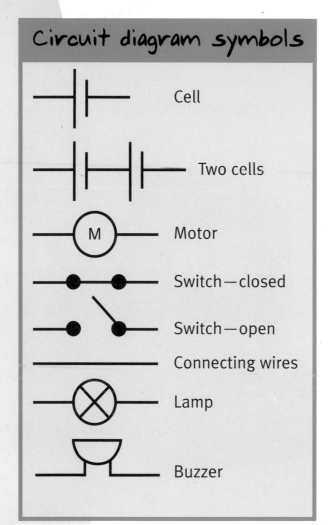

Circuit diagram symbols

	Cell
	Two cells
M	Motor
	Switch—closed
	Switch—open
	Connecting wires
	Lamp
	Buzzer

Scientists use symbols to draw pictures of circuits. These diagrams can be drawn quickly and are understood by other scientists.

Recording a circuit diagram

When scientists carry out an experiment, they also write up a report of what they have done. In the report, they may include diagrams. When a circuit diagram is drawn, scientists do not draw each component and the wires bending around them. They use symbols, as shown. They also draw the wires as straight lines connecting the components together. Some of the symbols for the components used in making circuits are shown here.

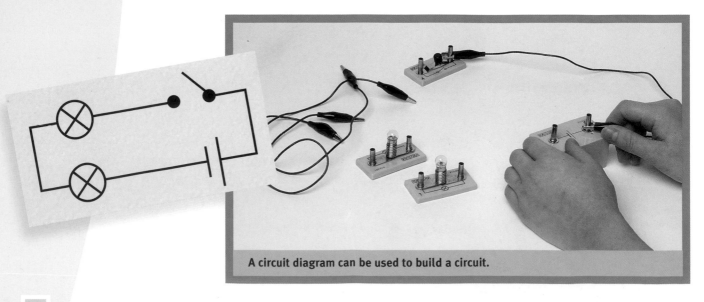

A circuit diagram can be used to build a circuit.

When cells make batteries

There are two vertical lines on the symbol for a cell. The long line stands for the positive terminal, and the short line stands for the negative terminal. When two or more cells are connected to a circuit, they make a battery. This is shown with the short line from one cell connected to the long line of the next cell.

This complicated circuit diagram shows the engineer how the circuit is connected.

Using circuit diagrams

Electrical devices, such as washing machines and televisions, have very complicated circuits to make them work. This means that the circuit diagrams are very complicated, too, but they can be understood by electrical engineers who build and repair them.

Understanding symbols

1 What are the components in this circuit?
2 What will happen when the switch is closed?
3 What would happen if one of the cells were removed and the switch closed?

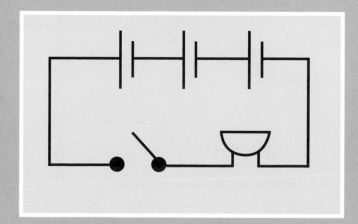

SWITCHES

**A switch controls the flow of electricity in a circuit.
When the switch is on, electricity can flow.
When the switch is off, the electricity cannot flow.**

Contacts

A switch has two pieces of metal in it with a gap between them. The ends of the pieces of metal on either side of the gap are called the contacts.

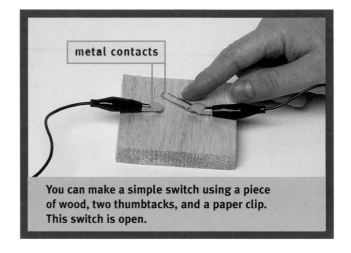

metal contacts

You can make a simple switch using a piece of wood, two thumbtacks, and a paper clip. This switch is open.

Closed and open switches

When a switch is on, scientists say that it is closed. The gap in the switch is closed by the metal contacts being brought together, so the current of electricity can flow. When a switch is off, scientists say that the switch is open. The metal contacts have been moved apart, and a gap has opened between them.

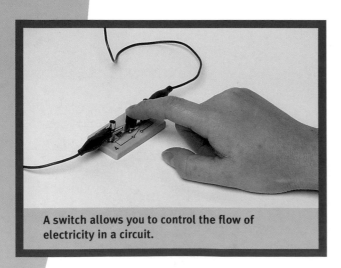

A switch allows you to control the flow of electricity in a circuit.

Why switches are used

If a circuit did not have a switch, the wires would have to be joined together and pulled apart to control the flow of electricity. This could damage them. Also, it would be too dangerous to pull apart wires and join them in a household circuit because the electricity is powerful enough to kill you.

Push switch

A push switch is used in a circuit with a doorbell. You push against a spring in the switch to close the gap and ring the bell. When you stop pushing, the spring opens the gap again, and the bell stops ringing.

Rocker switch

When one part of the rocker switch is pressed, the contacts are locked together, and the switch is closed. When the other part of the rocker is pressed, the contacts are locked apart, and the switch is open.

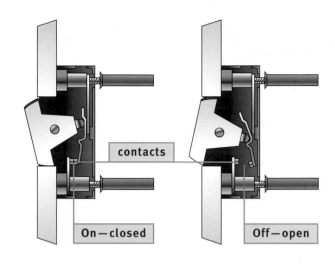

contacts

On—closed Off—open

A light switch on a wall is a rocker switch. The switch on the left is closed because the contacts are touching. The switch on the right is open.

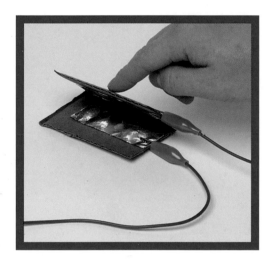

Pressure switch

A pressure switch works by having two contacts with a gap between them. If the switch is pressed, the contacts come together to close the switch. Many types of burglar alarms have a pressure switch that is placed under the carpet. When a burglar stands on the carpet, the pressure of his or her weight pushing on the contacts brings them together and closes the switch.

Different switches

Look around for different types of switches. Count the number of push switches, rocker switches, and pressure switches you find. Rocker switches have an on and off position; push switches are like doorbells. Draw a bar graph to show your results. Which switch was found the most often?

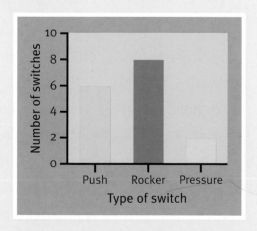

LAMPS IN CIRCUITS

If you look into the bulb of a lamp when it is switched off, you can see a wire inside it. When electricity flows through a circuit, only the wire in the lamp lights up. This is because the wire in the bulb is made from a special type of metal called tungsten.

The wire in a bulb is coiled so that a long length can fit inside it and provide a large amount of light.

What happens when electricity flows

Metals contain tiny particles called electrons. These electrons are free to move around. When a metal wire is put into a circuit and the circuit is switched on, electricity makes the electrons all move in the same direction, the way people do when going to a football game.

Why a lamp lights up

The electrons use up energy as they move along the wires in a circuit. When they reach the wire in a lamp, they have a problem. This wire does not let them pass through it as easily. It resists the movement of the electrons, the way a narrow hallway holds up a crowd trying to pass through it. We say it has a high resistance.

As the electrons push their way through this wire, they use up lots of energy. Some of this energy becomes heat and light energy. This makes the wire glow and become hot.

Two lamps in a row

If two lamps are connected into a circuit in a row, they are said to be "in series." When electricity flows through them, the resistance of the wire in one lamp adds to the resistance of the wire in the second lamp. This makes it even more difficult for the electrons to move along the wire. They move more slowly and push with less energy, and as a result, both lamps glow less brightly.

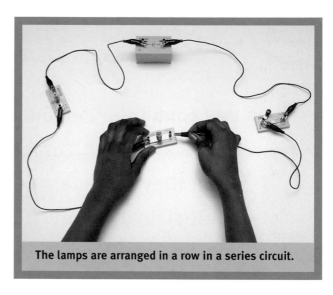

The lamps are arranged in a row in a series circuit.

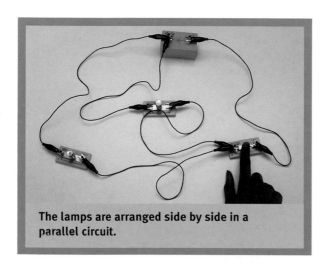

The lamps are arranged side by side in a parallel circuit.

Two lamps side by side

If two lamps are connected into a circuit side by side, they are said to be "in parallel." When electricity flows through them, the resistance of the wire in one lamp does not add to the resistance of the wire in the second lamp. The electrons push through as if there was only one lamp in the circuit, and both lamps shine brightly.

Brighter or dimmer

1 Will the lamps be brighter, dimmer, or the same as two lamps in series?

2 Will the lamps be brighter, dimmer, or the same as two lamps in parallel?

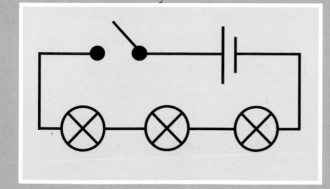

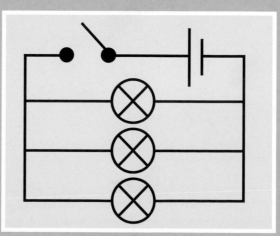

CHANGING CELLS AND LAMPS

A cell supplies a certain amount of electrical power. Lamps work best when they receive a certain amount of electrical power. If they receive too much power, they quickly burn out.

Looking for the voltage

The power supplied by a cell is measured in volts and is called the voltage. The voltage of a cell is written on its side, as explained on page 7. The power at which a component, such as a lamp, works best is written on its side, too.

The voltages are marked on some of the components of a circuit.

Increasing the power

The power in a circuit can be increased by adding cells in series. For example, putting two 1.5 V cells in a circuit increases the voltage to 1.5 + 1.5 = 3.0 V.

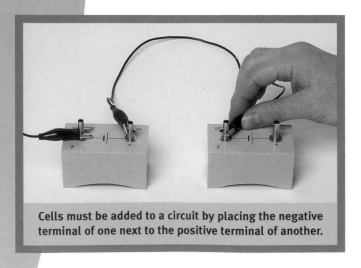

Cells must be added to a circuit by placing the negative terminal of one next to the positive terminal of another.

When a voltage is too low

If a component is supplied with a lower voltage than it needs, it does not work well. For example, a lamp only glows dimly or a motor turns slowly. Increasing the voltage in a circuit can increase the performance of the component, but there is a danger of it burning out.

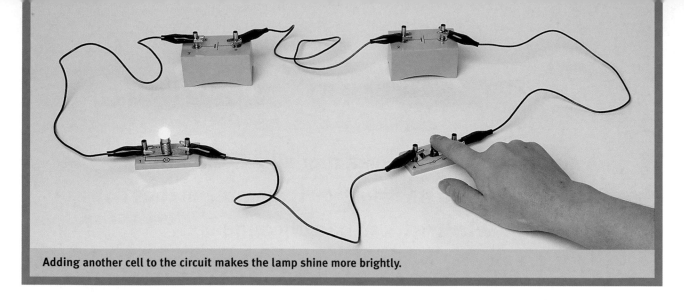

Adding another cell to the circuit makes the lamp shine more brightly.

When a voltage is too high

If a component is provided with a higher voltage than it needs, the wire inside it becomes very hot and melts. This makes a gap in the circuit, and the electricity stops flowing. The heat may also cause other parts of the component, such as a plastic covering, to melt. This can be very dangerous.

Increasing performance

A 4.5 V lamp will glow dimly with a 1.5 V cell in the circuit but will shine very brightly with three 1.5 V cells (that is 4.5 V) in the circuit. If four 1.5 V cells (6.0 V) are in the circuit, the lamp will shine very brightly and then go out when the wire in the bulb melts.

Decreasing performance

A 4.5 V lamp in a circuit with three 1.5 V cells can be made to shine less brightly by removing a cell. It can also be made to shine less brightly by adding a second lamp in series with it. This increases the resistance to the flow of electricity in the circuit (see page 13).

Dim, bright, or burn out?

The table shows five circuits with the voltage of the cells and the voltage of a lamp in the circuit. What do you think will happen to each lamp when the circuit is switched on?

Circuit	Voltage of cells	Voltage of lamp
A	3.0	1.5
B	3.0	3.0
C	4.5	6.0
D	1.5	4.5
E	6.0	3.0

CONDUCTORS AND INSULATORS

A conductor is a material that allows electricity to pass through it. An insulator is a material that does not allow electricity to pass through it.

Conductors in a circuit

All of the components in a circuit have metal in them that conducts electricity around the circuit.

Testing materials

We can test materials to see if they are conductors or insulators using a simple circuit.

A circuit with a cell, a lamp, a switch, and a gap is used to make the test. The switch is opened, and the material to be tested is placed across the gap so that it touches the ends of both wires. The switch is then closed, and the lamp is observed. If the lamp lights, the material is a conductor. If the lamp does not light, the material is an insulator.

buzzer

lamp

motor

All of these components contain metal conductors through which electricity can pass.

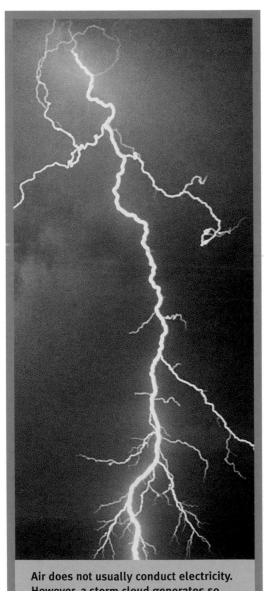

Air does not usually conduct electricity. However, a storm cloud generates so much electricity that the air around it changes into a conductor and a current passes through it as lightning.

Conductors

When steel, copper, aluminum, and iron are put across the gap, the lamp glows. This shows that they are conductors. If the column of graphite from inside a pencil is put across the gap, the lamp glows, too. Graphite is not a metal, but it does conduct electricity.

Insulators

When wood, plastic, or pottery is put across the gap, the components do not work. This shows that these materials are insulators. They are also not metals.

Air acts as an insulator

If there is a gap in a circuit, air fills it. Air is usually an insulator. If you fail to connect the wires in a circuit securely to a component, they may fall away and a gap may develop, which stops the flow of electricity. This is why it is very important to check all of the wire connections if a circuit does not work properly.

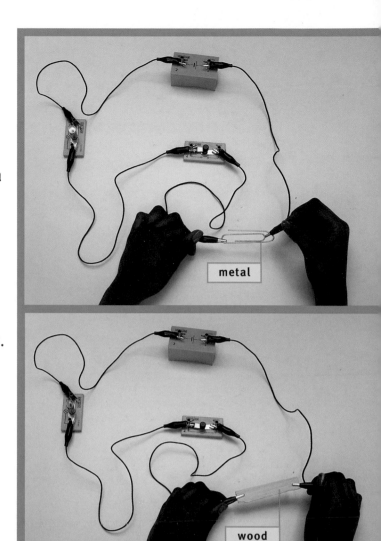

You can tell if the material in the gap is a conductor or insulator by looking at the lamp when the switch is closed.

What were the materials?

Five materials were tested in a circuit. A check mark means that the lamp lit up; an X means that it did not light up.

1 Which materials were conductors?

2 Which materials were insulators?

3 Which materials were probably metals?

4 Which materials were not metals?

Material	Lamp
A	✓
B	X
C	✓
D	X
E	X

CHANGING RESISTANCE

Every conductor offers some resistance to the flow of electricity. The resistance acts to stop the current of electricity from flowing as strongly.

The resistance in the lighting circuit in a movie theater is increased when the lights are dimmed.

Resistance and thickness

The electrons flowing in a circuit move through a conductor like water moving through a pipe. If a pipe is wide, a large volume of water can pass through, but if the pipe is narrow, only a small volume can pass through. In a similar way, a thick conductor can let more electrons pass through it than a thin conductor can. This means that a thick conductor offers less resistance to a current of electricity than a thin conductor does.

Resistance and length

The resistance of a wire in a circuit also depends on its length. A short wire has a small amount of metal in it to offer resistance. A long wire has more metal to offer resistance. A short, thick wire would make the best conductor.

Changing the number of lamps

The resistance in a circuit can also be increased by adding more lamps in a series. The metal in the filament of a lamp has a high resistance (see page 12). Each one offers further resistance to the flow of electricity in the circuit.

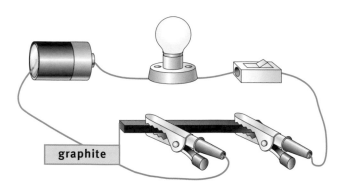

graphite

The resistance in the circuit of this stereo is reduced when the volume is turned up.

Variable resistors

A device that has a length of conductor that can be varied, such as the graphite in the picture, is called a variable resistor. You can change the length of the graphite in the circuit by moving the alligator clips. If you move the clips farther apart, the length of graphite increases and the lamp becomes dimmer. If you move the clips closer together, the length of graphite in the circuit decreases and the lamp shines more brightly. Variable resistors are used in the volume control of a radio or television. They are also used in dimmer switches in homes and movie theaters.

How the lamps changed

A variable resistor was placed in a circuit with a lamp. Different lengths of the resistor were put into the circuit, and the light shining from the lamp was noted. What do you think was written in the three empty boxes in the table?

Length of wire inches (cm)	Brightness of bulb
4 (10 cm)	very bright
8 (20 cm)	
12 (30 cm)	
16 (40 cm)	

HOUSEHOLD ELECTRICITY

Household electricity is used in all kinds of buildings and outside, too, such as in street lights. It is much more powerful than the electricity produced by cells and batteries and can be used for a wide range of tasks.

Lighting

Lightbulbs and fluorescent tubes are the two most common forms of lighting. You can find out why a wire in a lightbulb gives off light on page 12. A fluorescent tube, such as the lights in schools and offices, has a gas called mercury vapor inside it, which is a conductor. This gas gives off energy as rays when it conducts electricity. The rays strike chemicals called phosphors in the tube wall and make them shine. Many street lights have a gas called sodium vapor in them. This is a conductor, too. When electricity passes through this gas, it shines with a bright orange-yellow light.

Electricity provides the light for rooms in buildings and for people traveling along the streets.

Heating

Electricity is used to provide heat. There is a coil of wire called a heating element in an electric heater. The coil of wire has a very high resistance. The heating element releases energy as heat when a current passes through it. A hair dryer has a heating element and an electric motor in it. The motor spins a fan, which blows air over the element to make the air hot so that you can dry your hair.

The electric motor in a hair dryer spins a fan, which blows air over a heating element to make the air hot.

Movement

An electric motor can make things move. Inside a motor is a coil of wire. When a current of electricity passes into the coil, it makes the coil act like a magnet, which makes it spin. The center of the coil is connected to a shaft that also spins. It is the spinning shaft that provides movement to the wheels of a model car, the turntable in a CD player, the paper moving through a computer printer, or a food mixer.

Comparing power

The power needed to make an electrical device work is measured in watts. The symbol is W.

1 Which device uses the most power?
2 Which device uses the least power?
3 What is the difference in power used between a television and a lightbulb?
4 What is the difference in power used between an iron and an electric drill?

Electrical device	Power (W)
Lightbulb	60
Television	200
Electric heater	2,000
Refrigerator	150
Iron	700
Electric drill	360

ELECTRICAL SAFETY

The human body is a conductor of electricity. If a large amount of electricity passes into it, the electricity can burn the skin, cause an electric shock, and even kill. Great care must be taken with electricity.

All electrical devices have instruction booklets. These children are following the instructions to use the computers safely.

Plugs

An appliance should be switched off before it is unplugged. The cable should not be tugged to pull the plug out of the outlet.

Do not use adaptors to plug a large number of plugs into one socket. This causes a large current to be drawn. Because a large current produces a large amount of heat, the current could cause the plugs and cables to catch fire.

Cables

Cables must not be put under rugs and carpets, where they may wear away unseen. They must be kept in view so that any damage can be seen easily. Damaged cables must not be used.

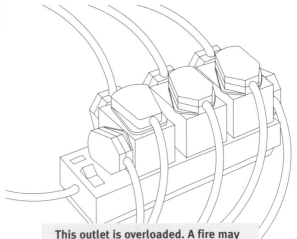

This outlet is overloaded. A fire may start if it is turned on.

Water

Water conducts electricity, so you must never handle electrical equipment with wet hands or near water. Do not touch a switch if you have wet hands because water may flow to the contacts and conduct a current to you. The cord of a pull switch in a bathroom is made from insulating material, which prevents electricity from the switch from reaching your hands. Devices that use household electricity must not be taken into the bathroom in case you touch them with wet hands.

Substations have warning signs to keep people away from them.

Power lines

Kites must not be flown near overhead power lines. If a kite becomes stuck on a power line, electricity may pass down the string to the person holding it and give the person a large electric shock, which could kill him or her.

Substations

A substation delivers electricity to a neighborhood and is surrounded by a high fence. Children should not climb over the fence to play on the substation because they may receive a fatal electric shock.

Electrical safety

Read the scenarios below and decide whether you think the people did the right thing or not. What would you do in that situation?

1 Children playing football accidentally throw the ball into a substation. One boy climbs the fence to get the ball back.

2 A woman is changing a lightbulb in a lamp. She unplugs the lamp before she removes the bulb and replaces it with a new one.

POWER STATIONS

Household electricity is generated at a power station. Many power stations use energy from fuel to generate electricity. Some use energy from the wind or from flowing water.

Generating electricity

Electricity is produced in a generator. Steam from a boiler pushes on turbine blades and makes them spin. This makes a magnet spin inside coils of wire. Currents of electricity flow in the coils and are conducted away on cables to towns and cities.

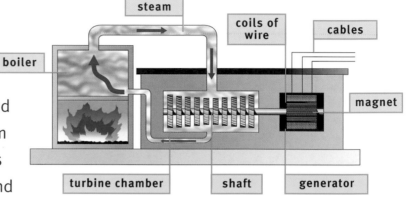

steam • coils of wire • cables • boiler • magnet • turbine chamber • shaft • generator

A power station that burns fossil fuels has three main parts: the boiler, turbine chamber, and generator.

Power station fuels

Many power stations burn fossil fuels—coal, gas, or oil—to release heat energy and make steam. Burning fossil fuels causes large amounts of harmful gases to be released into the air. This may cause global warming and acid rain, which can damage buildings, plants, and fish. Some power stations use nuclear fuel. When nuclear fuel is made, it produces harmful rays called radiation. Great care is taken to stop the radiation from escaping from the power station. The energy released from fuels is used to heat water and make steam.

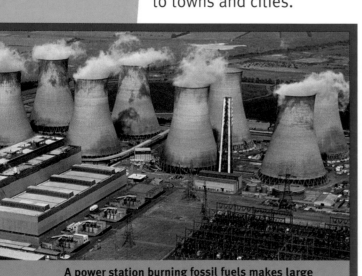

A power station burning fossil fuels makes large clouds of smoke that contains harmful gases.

Water and wind

Some power stations use flowing water to spin the turbine blades. These power stations, called hydroelectric power stations, have a dam built across a river. The water collects behind the dam and is then released through the turbines.

A wind farm is built in a place where strong winds blow for most of the year. Each generator on the farm is mounted on a tall column and has two or more turbine blades attached to it. The wind pushes on the blades and spins them.

Saving energy

Eventually, fossil and nuclear fuels will be used up, so new ways of generating electricity need to be found. More power stations using renewable energy, such as wind and moving water, may be developed. In the meantime, you can help save fuel by switching off all electrical equipment when it is not in use.

The turbines make noise and are easily seen in the countryside, but they do not damage the environment by producing harmful gases.

Comparing power stations

The bar graph shows the percentage of electrical power provided by different kinds of power stations in a country.

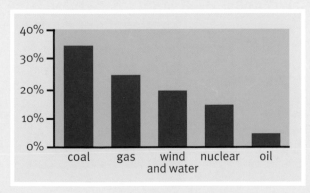

1 Which kind of power station produced the most electrical power?

2 Which kind of power station produced the least electrical power?

3 What percentage of electricity was produced from a fuel that has harmful rays?

4 What percentage of power was produced by power stations that affect global warming?

CAN YOU REMEMBER THE ESSENTIALS?

Here you can learn all of the essential science facts about circuits and conductors. They are presented in the order you read about them in the book. Spend a couple of minutes learning each set of facts. If you can learn all of them, you know all of the essentials about circuits and conductors.

Introduction (pages 4–5)

Electricity flows in a loop called a circuit.
A battery contains a store of electrical energy.
Electricity flows around a circuit through electrical conductors.
The items that are linked together in a circuit are called components.

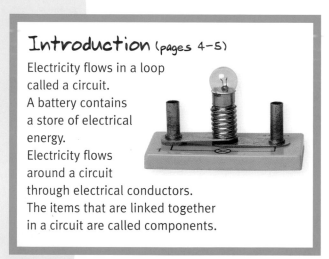

Symbols (pages 8–9)

Each component in a diagram has a symbol. The symbols of components can be joined together to make a circuit diagram.

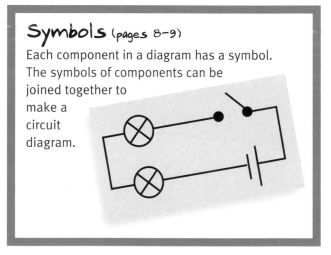

Batteries and cells (pages 6–7)

A cell contains chemicals that can generate electricity.
A group of cells make a battery.
A current flows from a cell's negative terminal to the positive terminal.

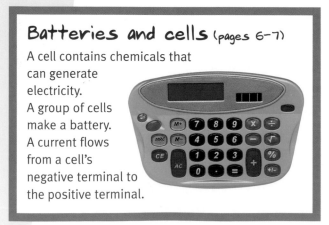

Switches (pages 10–11)

A switch controls the flow of electricity in a circuit.
A closed switch allows electricity to flow.
An open switch stops electricity from flowing.

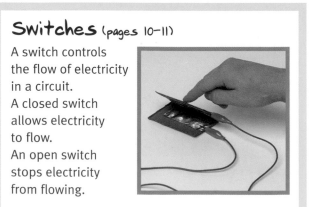

Lamps in circuits (pages 12-13)

A lamp has a metal filament that has a high resistance. When electricity passes through the filament, the filament glows.
Lamps arranged in a row are said to be in series.
Lamps arranged side by side are said to be in parallel.

Protecting circuits (pages 20-21)

Too large a current in a wire can cause a fire. If wiring is damaged, a large current can flow in a short circuit.
A fuse protects a circuit against a large current.

Changing cells and lamps (pages 14-15)

The power of a cell to push a current is measured in volts. The voltage in a circuit can be increased by adding cells.
Components work best at a certain voltage. If a component receives electricity at too high a voltage, it burns out.

Household electricity (pages 22-23)

Household electricity can provide light. Household electricity can provide heat. Electric motors change the energy in electricity into movement.

Conductors and insulators (pages 16-17)

A conductor is a material that allows electricity to pass through it. An insulator is a material that does not allow electricity to pass through it. Metals and graphite are conductors.
Wood, plastic, and pottery are insulators.

Electrical safety (pages 24-25)

Electricity can kill. Never touch electrical equipment or switches with wet hands. Do not overload outlets. Keep away from overhead power lines and substations.

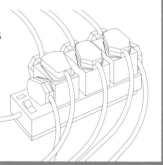

Changing resistance (pages 18-19)

If the resistance is high, a small current can flow. If the resistance is low, a large current can flow. The resistance of a wire can be varied by altering its length or thickness.

Power stations (pages 26-27)

Electricity is produced in a generator in a power station.
Many power stations use fuels.
Some power stations use flowing water.
Wind is used to produce electricity at a wind farm.

GLOSSARY

Amp A unit used to measure electric currents.

Battery A group of cells joined together.

Cable A large, thick wire that conducts electricity overhead. A group of thick wires coated in insulation material that conducts electricity underground. A small number of thin wires coated in plastic that are used to connect electrical devices such as computers and printers to outlets and to each other.

Cell A metal cylinder containing chemicals that can make electricity flow in a circuit when the switch in the circuit is closed.

Circuit A loop made by connecting electrical components together so that a current of electricity can pass through them.

Conductor A material that allows an electric current to pass through it.

Contact A piece of metal in a switch that is made to touch a second contact so that electricity can flow in a circuit.

Current The flow of electricity in a circuit.

Electrons Tiny particles inside conductors that move in one direction when a circuit is switched on and make the current of electricity.

Energy Something that allows an object or a living thing to take part in an activity such as moving or giving out light.

Filament A thin wire with many coils used in a lamp to provide light when electricity flows through it.

Fuel A material that releases energy that can be used to make machines, such as electrical generators, work.

Fuse A device with a metal wire in it that melts and breaks if a large current passes through it.

Generator A machine that produces a current of electricity.

Graphite A material made from a black substance called carbon.

In parallel The arrangement of components that are wired side by side in a circuit.

In series The arrangement of components that are wired in a row in a circuit.

Insulator A material that does not allow a current of electricity to pass through it.

Irreversible change A change that takes place when a material changes and cannot be turned back again to the original material.

Metal A substance with a shiny surface that conducts electricity.

Phosphors Materials that give off light when struck by rays made inside a fluorescent lamp.

Resistance A property of a conductor that slows down the flow of electricity through it.

Terminal A point on a cell or battery where a wire is connected to form a circuit.

Variable resistor A device that can control the amount of electricity flowing through a circuit by altering its resistance.

Voltage The power of a cell, battery, or generator to produce electricity. Voltage is measured in volts (V).

Watts A unit used to measure power (W).

ANSWERS

Batteries and cells (pages 6–7)

B and D

Symbols (pages 8–9)

1 Three cells, a switch, and a buzzer.
2 The buzzer will make a loud noise.
3 The buzzer will make a quieter noise.

Switches (pages 10–11)

Rocker switch.

Lamps in circuits (pages 12–13)

1 Dimmer.
2 The same.

Changing cells and lamps (pages 14–15)

A Shine very brightly, then burn out.
B Shine very brightly.
C Shine brightly.
D Shine dimly.
E Shine very brightly, then burn out.

Conductors and insulators (pages 16–17)

1 A and C.
2 B, D, and E.
3 A and C.
4 B, D, and E.

Changing resistance (pages 18–19)

8 inches (20 cm)—bright.
12 inches (30 cm)—dim.
16 inches (40 cm)—very dim.

Protecting circuits (pages 20–21)

B, D, C, A.

Household electricity (pages 22–23)

1 Electric heater.
2 Lightbulb.
3 140 W.
4 340 W.

Electrical safety (pages 24–25)

1 Wrong—the boy should have left the ball where it was because it is dangerous to go near substations.
2 Right—the woman stays safe by turning off the flow of electricity to the lamp before changing the bulb.

Power stations (pages 26–27)

1 Coal-fired power station.
2 Oil-fired power station.
3 15%.
4 65%.

INDEX